How to Prepare For the CAT/6*

* CAT/ 6 is a registered trademark of Educational Testing Service, which was not involved in the production of and does not endorse this product

3rd Grade Edition

By John Weingarten

carney
EDUCATIONAL SERVICES

CARNEY EDUCATIONAL SERVICES
Helping Students Help Themselves

This book is dedicated to:

The moms and dads who get up early and stay up late. You are the true heroes, saving our future, one precious child at a time.

All the kids who don't make the evening news. To the wide-eyed children, full of love, energy, and wonder. You are as close to perfection as this world will ever see.

TABLE OF CONTENTS

3rd Grade Edition

An Overview of the CAT/6 Test

In the spring of 2002, the California Department of Education adopted the California Achievement Test, Sixth Edition (the CAT/6) as part of the state's Standardized Testing and Reporting System (STAR). The purpose behind this test is to provide California public school districts and parents with information about how their children are performing compared with other public school children from across the state. Keep in mind that this is a test of basic skills. It was written to assess the abilities of students only in specified areas of the curriculum. The CAT/6 is a standardized test, meaning that all public school children across California take the tests in the same manner and during the same months of the school year period. The directions given by teachers are the same, as are the amounts of time given to complete each testing section.

Why did California change from the SAT 9 to the CAT/6?

Over the last several years, the Stanford 9 (also referred to as SAT 9) standardized tests had generated controversy in some school districts due to errors in data analysis. Some of the important information reported by school districts was misused or analyzed incorrectly. These errors became quite costly to identify and correct. Additionally, some districts with large numbers of non-English speaking students encouraged parents to request waivers which would exclude their children from taking the SAT 9. Obviously, districts which sought to exclude such students from taking the test would receive higher scores than those districts which sought to test every student. In changing to the CAT/6, the California Board of Education decided to use a test with much more of a history in the state. The California Aptitude Tests were first developed in 1950, and are currently in use in nine other states. The CAT/6 will be administered by the Educational Testing Service (ETS), which is the largest testing firm in the nation.

What does the CAT/6 seek to measure?

Beginning in the spring of 2003, approximately 4.5 million students in grades 2-11 will be taking multiple choice tests in two main areas of the curriculum: Mathematics and Language Arts. The specific skills tested within Language Arts are vocabulary, reading comprehension, spelling, language mechanics (grammar), and language expression (word usage). The math sections of the test measure student mastery of math computation, math concepts and math applications. Students in grades 4-12 may be given a study skills subtest, which will measure how well student scan use information processing skills which they can use across all subject areas. The CAT test series also contains science and social studies subtests, but whether these will be used as part of the STAR program has yet to be determined.

Why do schools give standardized tests?

The CAT/6 gives schools an idea of how well they are teaching basic skills which all students need to be successful in the future. These skills are defined for schools in documents called "State Standards." The State Department of Education has spelled out for teachers, parents and students what they should be learning in each academic subject during a given school year. Schools receive data about how their students performed both individually and by grade level. Which state standards did students meet? Which standards need to be taught differently next year? How can schools help each child move toward meeting all the standards? All of these questions can be best answered by using the data provided by the CAT/6. Standardized tests are valuable because they are an objective way to measure how successfully schools are delivering the basics. The idea behind standardizing the test is this: if every public school student takes the same tests in the same way, then it is a fair way to compare schools and districts. If, for example, one school gave children an extra 5 hours to complete the test, then it would be an unfair advantage given to those children.

What about criticism of standardized tests?

In the last few years, criticism of standardized tests has mounted. Many parents and teachers say that preparing for these tests takes away time from valuable subjects like art, drama and music. They have also noted the stressful nature of these tests and question whether it is healthy to subject young children to this type of pressure to perform. Others believe these tests reward wealthy school districts in the suburbs, while they punish inner-city school districts with large numbers of non-English speaking students. While some of these criticisms are valid, they do not change the fact that standardized tests are widely regarded as the best way for schools to measure how they are teaching to the California State Standards. As long as the public asks public schools to prove they are doing an effective job educating children, these tests will be with us. The criticism of the Stanford 9 test resulted in replacing it with the CAT/6, which is ANOTHER standardized test.

As parents, we need to realize that these tests have become a fact of life in California public schools and help children prepare for them. Certainly, schools and teachers are primarily responsible for preparing your child for these tests. Yet parents have an important role to play. This book will give you many valuable tools you can use in helping your child do their best on this very important standardized test. It is the job of California public schools to teach to the standards, which are tested on the CAT/6, but your role as a reinforcer of skills and a supporter of your child's progress as a student cannot be ignored.

How Your Child Can Improve His/Her Score On ANY
Multiple Choice Standardized Test

Your child has entered an educational world that is run by standardized tests. Students take the Scholastic Aptitude Test (SAT) to help them get into college and the Graduate Record Examination (GRE) to help them get into graduate school. Other exams like the ACT and the PSAT are not as well-known, but also very important to your child's future success. Schools spend a great deal of time teaching children the material they need to know to do well on these tests, but very little time teaching children HOW to take these tests. This is a gap that parents can easily fill. To begin with, you can look for opportunities to strengthen your child's reading and vocabulary skills as well as his/her ability to follow detailed written directions.

The importance of reading:

Students who do well on standardized tests tend to be excellent readers. They read frequently for pleasure and have a good understanding of what they have read. You can help support your child as a reader by helping him/her set aside a regular time to read each and every day. As you may know, children tend to be successful when they follow an established pattern of behavior. Even 15-20 minutes spent reading a magazine or newspaper before bedtime will help. Children should read both fiction and non-fiction material at home, as well as at school. Ask your child about what s/he has read. Help him/her to make connections between a book s/he is currently reading and a movie or a television show s/he has recently seen. THE BOTTOM LINE: Children who read well will do better on the test than children who do not. There is written material in all sections of the test that must be quickly comprehended. Even the math sections have written information contained in each question.

The importance of building a larger vocabulary:

As you may know, children who read well and who read often tend to have a large vocabulary. This is important since there is an entire section of the test that is devoted exclusively to the use of vocabulary words. You can support your child in attempting to improve his/her vocabulary by encouraging him/her to read challenging material on a regular basis. The newspaper is a good place to start. Studies have shown that many newspaper articles are written on a 4th to 5th grade reading level! Help your child to use new and more difficult words both in his/her own conversations and in his/her writings. If you use an advanced vocabulary when speaking to your children, don't be surprised if they begin to incorporate some of the new words into his/her daily speech. One of the most immediate ways to judge the intelligence of anyone is in his/her use of language. Children are aware of this too. THE BOTTOM LINE: Children who have an expansive vocabulary will do better on the test than children who do not. Find as many ways as possible to help build new words into your child's speech and writing.

The importance of following written directions:

The test is a teacher-directed test. Teachers tell students how to complete each section of the test and give them specific examples that are designed to help them understand what to do. However, teachers are not allowed to help students once each test has begun. The written script for teachers seems to repeat one phrase continually: "READ THE DIRECTIONS CAREFULLY." This is certainly not an accident. Students face a series of questions that cannot be answered correctly unless they clearly understand what is being asked. Help your child by giving him/her a series of tasks to complete at home in writing. Directions should be multi-step and should be as detailed as possible without frustrating your child. For example: "Please take out the trash cans this afternoon. Place all the bottles and cans in the blue recycling bin and place all the extra newspapers that are stacked in the garage in the yellow recycling bin." If children are able to follow these types of directions and are able to reread to clarify what is being asked, they will be at a tremendous advantage when it comes to the test.
THE BOTTOM LINE: Children who are able to follow a series of detailed, written directions will have a tremendous advantage over those who are unable to do so.

All of the previous suggestions are designed to be used before the test is actually given to help your child improve in some basic test-taking skills. Here are some strategies that you can teach your child to use once s/he is taking the test:

1. SELECT THE BEST ANSWER.

The test, like many multiple-choice tests, isn't designed for children to write their own answers to the questions. They will fill in a bubble by the four answer choices and select the BEST possible answer. Reading the question carefully is quite important, since the question may contain key words needed to select the correct answer. For example:

The first President of the United States was

a. John Adams.
b. James Madison.
c. George Washington.
d. Thomas Jefferson.

The correct answer is, of course, "c". Students would need to read the question carefully and focus on the key word in the question: "first". All of the names listed were Presidents of the United States early in our history, but only choice "c" contains the name of our first President. Looking for key words like "least" or "greater" will help your child to select the best answer from among the choices given.

2. ANSWER THE EASY QUESTIONS FIRST.

The test contains a series of timed tests. Children who waste time on a difficult question found at the beginning of a test may run out of time before they finish the entire test. A good strategy is to skip anything that seems too difficult to answer immediately. Once your children have answered every "easy" question in the section, they can go back through the test and spend more time working on the more time-consuming questions. If students are given only 30 minutes to answer 25 reading vocabulary questions, they shouldn't spend much more than a minute on each one. Wasting four or five minutes on one question is not a good idea, since it reduces the amount of time your child will have to work on the rest of the test. Once time runs out, that's it! Any questions left unanswered will be counted wrong when the test is machine scored. Working on the easier questions first will allow your child to make the best use of the allowed time.

3. ELIMINATE ANY UNREASONABLE ANSWER CHOICES.

No matter how intelligent your child is, it is inevitable that s/he will come to a test question that s/he finds too difficult to answer. In this situation, the best thing to do is to make an "educated guess." If students can eliminate one or more of the answer choices given, they have a much greater chance of answering the question correctly.

For example:

Select the word below that means the same as the underlined word:

Jennifer became <u>enraged</u> when she found out her diary had been read.

    a. mournful
    b. furious
    c. pleased
    d. depressed

Even if your child didn't know that "b" is the best answer choice, s/he could certainly eliminate choice "c" from consideration. Clearly, Jennifer would not be "pleased" to find out her diary had been read.

4. DO MATH QUESTIONS ON PAPER WHEN NECESSARY.

The math sections of the test cause children problems because several of the answer choices seem like they could be correct. The only way to select the best answer choice for some math questions is to do the math calculation on scratch paper. The answer choices given for these questions are written to discourage guessing.

For example:

Eileen has saved $3245 to buy a car. Her aunt gave her another $250 as a gift. How much does she have in all?

    a. $3595
    b. $4495
    c. $3495
    d. $3485

The correct answer is "c", but it is hard to select the correct answer because all of the answer choices seem similar. The best way to determine the correct answer would be to add $3245 and $250 on scratch paper.

If you work with your children with these simple strategies, you will find that they will approach these tests with confidence, rather than with anxiety. Teach your children to prepare and then to approach the test with a positive attitude. They should be able to say to themselves, "I know this stuff, I'll do a great job today."

READING VOCABULARY

Content Cluster: SYNONYMS

Objective: To evaluate knowledge of word choice and meaning.

Parent Tip: One of the best ways to build your child's vocabulary is to read challenging text with them. Discuss with your child any difficult words you may encounter together, and suggest simpler vocabulary for those words.

Select a synonym to match the <u>underlined</u> word.

Example: An <u>avenue</u> is a

    a.   driveway
    b.   stairs
    c.   street
    d.   ramp

The correct answer is "c". Street is a synonym for avenue.

1.   <u>Secret</u> means

    a.   open
    b.   known
    c.   private
    d.   free

2.   To <u>imitate</u> someone is to

    a.   hurt
    b.   look at
    c.   bother
    d.   copy

3.   To <u>preserve</u> means to

    a.   buy
    b.   sell
    c.   save
    d.   yell

4.   <u>Replace</u> means

     a.   to move
     b.   to jump
     c.   to put back
     d.   to scream

5.   A <u>blizzard</u> is a

     a.   reptile
     b.   storm
     c.   rainy day
     d.   sunny day

Content Cluster: MULTIPLE MEANINGS

Objective: To evaluate recognition of words with multiple meanings and to identify meaning in context.

Parent Tip: Help your child understand that many words in the English language have more than one meaning. It is important to know how to use the words appropriately.

Directions: Choose the sentence that has the same meaning as the underlined word in the given sentence.

Example: In which sentence does the word <u>hand</u> mean the same thing as in the following sentence?

I put the apple in her <u>hand</u>.

    a.   On one <u>hand</u>, she liked camp.
    b.   Can you <u>hand</u> me a box of crayons?
    c.   She held her mom's <u>hand</u> when she crossed the street.
    d.   The baseball player heard the fans giving him a <u>hand</u>.

The correct answer is "c". Hand is the same in both sentences.

1.   In which sentence does the word <u>last</u> mean the same thing as in the following sentence?

    What is your <u>last</u> name?

    a.   We played baseball <u>last</u> year.
    b.   The boy was <u>last</u> in line.
    c.   How long does recess <u>last</u>?
    d.   She took one <u>last</u> look around the house.

2.   In which sentence does the word <u>back</u> mean the same thing as in the following sentence?

    She played basketball in the <u>back</u> parking lot.

    a.   Jan's <u>back</u> hurt from gymnastics class.
    b.   Vivian came <u>back</u> from her vacation.
    c.   You must <u>back</u> your car out of the driveway.
    d.   Shana was in the <u>back</u> of the lunch line.

3. In which sentence does the word <u>wave</u> mean the same thing as in the following sentence?

    The boat sailed over the <u>wave</u>.

    a.   The ocean <u>wave</u> crashed upon the shore.
    b.   I can <u>wave</u> to my friend in the audience.
    c.   She has a curly <u>wave</u> in her hair.
    d.   The trees <u>wave</u> in the wind.

4. In which sentence does the word <u>play</u> mean the same thing as in the following sentence?

    Two of my friends <u>play</u> the piano.

    a.   The students <u>play</u> kickball at recess.
    b.   We saw a great <u>play</u> last week!
    c.   I <u>play</u> at my friend's every day.
    d.   We like to <u>play</u> in the orchestra.

5. In which sentence does the word <u>check</u> mean the same thing as in the following sentence?

    The little girl will <u>check</u> under her bed for monsters.

    a.   After dinner we will pay our <u>check</u>.
    b.   Mom wrote a <u>check</u> for the video game.
    c.   Place a <u>check</u> next to the right answer.
    d.   You should <u>check</u> your answers again.

Content Cluster: CONTEXT

Objective: To evaluate knowledge of word meaning using sentence context.

Parent Tip: It is important to help your child understand that the meaning to an unfamiliar word is often found in the rest of the sentence. If your child attempts to sound out the word but is unsuccessful, have him/her complete the sentence. Reading the entire sentence will often provide a hint to the unknown word's meaning.

Directions: Find the word or words below that means the same or almost the same as the underlined word.

Example: The girl is so <u>charming</u> that everyone likes her. <u>Charming</u> means

    a.   mean
    b.   likeable
    c.   fantastic
    d.   good

The correct answer is "b". Charming means likeable.

1.   The animals were in the <u>meadow</u>. <u>Meadow</u> means

    a.   barn
    b.   mountains
    c.   field
    d.   forest

2.   The fire burned <u>brightly</u>. <u>Brightly</u> means

    a.   angrily
    b.   giving much light
    c.   smartly
    d.   carefully

3.   Lucy <u>concealed</u> her joy when she opened her present. <u>Concealed</u> means

    a.   yelled
    b.   loved
    c.   liked
    d.   hid

4.   The kind old lady was <u>generous</u> to the poor people. <u>Generous</u> means

    a.   stealing
    b.   lying
    c.   giving
    d.   cheating

5.   The robber left <u>evidence</u> at the scene of the crime. <u>Evidence</u> means

    a.   food
    b.   proof
    c.   luggage
    d.   treasure

Reading Comprehension

Content Cluster: RECREATIONAL READING

Objective: To evaluate reading comprehension skills using recreational text.

Parent Tip: There are three types of passages often used in testing situations. One type of passage, recreational reading, is reading for enjoyment. Textual reading is expository material read for information. Reading non-fiction material such as biographies or an encyclopedia would be an example of textual material. Functional reading is material read in order to perform a task. Reading a recipe would be an example of functional reading. It can be helpful to read the questions before reading the passage. This helps your child know what information the questions are asking, and then to look for that information while reading the passage, rather than trying to absorb every word. As you read books with your child, stop and ask them questions like, "What do you think will happen next?", or "Why do you think the character did what he did?" This helps children think beyond the text to make meaning of what they are reading.

Directions: Read the passage and answer the following questions.

Joey Gets a Home

Joey spent the first five years of his life in one of the tougher areas of Los Angeles. He lived with his mom, his nine-year old sister, and his three-year old little brother. Joey's dad died when Joey was three years old. When he was five years old, Joey's mom died of cancer. Joey's mom knew about the cancer, but didn't have the money to pay for the medicine and cancer treatments.

When Joey's mom died, Joey and his brother and sister were placed in foster homes. Before Joey was seven years old, he had lived with three different foster families. The foster families never told Joey why he had to leave, so he always blamed himself when it didn't work out. Joey also didn't see much of his brother and sister, but he often wondered where they were and how they were doing.

One day, Joey was placed in a foster home with the Morton family. Mr. and Mrs. Morton had a son name Ross, who was two months younger than Joey. Ross was an only child. At first Joey was afraid the Morton's would send him away, just like the other families. But after a couple of days, Joey and Ross became good friends. Mr. and Mrs. Morton treated Joey like their own son.

When one year had gone by, the Mortons asked Joey if he would like to be adopted. Joey was shocked. He knew that the Mortons loved him, but he couldn't believe they wanted him to be a part of their family forever. Finally, in his heart, Joey felt like he was part of a real family!

1.   Why was Joey shocked?

    a.   The Mortons hurt Joey's feelings
    b.   Nobody had ever wanted to adopt him before
    c.   Joey didn't like the Mortons
    d.   Joey wanted to go back to the foster home

2.   What happened to Joey's dad?

    a.   He had cancer
    b.   He moved to another city
    c.   He died
    d.   He remarried

3.   You can guess from the story's ending that Joey

    a.   Went to live with his brother and sister
    b.   Ran away
    c.   Was placed in another foster home
    d.   Was adopted

4.   Which of these happened first?

    a.   Joey's mom died
    b.   Joey was put in a foster home
    c.   The Mortons asked Joey if they could adopt him
    d.   Joey played with Ross

5.   Which is probably not a reason why Joey and Ross might have become good friends?

    a.   They were about the same age
    b.   They played together
    c.   Joey was older than Ross
    d.   They lived in the same house

Directions: Read the passage and answer the following questions.

My Surprise Trip

One morning last summer, before my dad left for work, he told us to pack up for a two-week vacation at the beach. We were going to leave when he came home from work that evening. My sisters and I were so excited that we ran upstairs to pack without saying goodbye to Dad. When Dad came home that evening, he found us all packed up and ready to leave.

We traveled many miles. The car trip seemed to take forever, but we finally arrived at the beach. First, we checked into our hotel, then we went out to dinner at a neat restaurant. I had a hot dog, and my sisters both had hamburgers. After dinner we went back to our hotel, watched a scary movie, and went to sleep.

During the first week we played in the ocean, made sand castles that washed away when the tide came in, and buried each other in the sand. We also played paddleball, volleyball, and threw the frisbee all over the beach. My mom made sure we had plenty of sunscreen on every day. That way we wouldn't get sunburned.

On Saturday, Dad told us he had another surprise for us. My sisters and I wondered what it could be. We found out when we went to dinner that night. Grandma and Grandpa had come to stay with us all the way from New York. What a neat surprise! We hadn't seen them in over a year.

Finally, it was our last day at the beach, and my sisters and I were sad. Mom and Dad tried not to show it, but they were sad too. Grandma and Grandpa had to go back to New York, and we had to leave too. I was sad to leave, but I'll never forget the fun time we had on our vacation at the beach!

1.   In this story, *checked* means

   a.   to write a check
   b.   to look into
   c.   to sign in
   d.   to pay for

2.   Why do you think the trip took forever?

   a.   It was a long distance away
   b.   The kids were anxious to get there
   c.   They had plenty of car trouble
   d.   They had to stop many times along the way

3.   What was one thing the kids did in the morning at the beach?

   a.   Went to dinner
   b.   Watched a movie
   c.   Grandma and Grandpa came into town
   d.   They played in the water

4.   Which would not be a reason the boy might vacation at the beach again?

   a.   He could play games like frisbee.
   b.   He could go for a long drive.
   c.   He might see his grandparents.
   d.   He could build sandcastles.

5.   How old do you think the boy in the story might be?

   a.   18 years old
   b.   2 years old
   c.   8 years old
   d.   21 years old

Content Cluster: TEXTUAL READING

Objective: To evaluate reading comprehension skills using informational text.

Parent Tip: As your child reads a story or passage to you or with you, ask your child to restate the story or passage briefly in his/her own words. This will allow you to determine your child's comprehension level. Also, encourage your child to ask the question, "Does this make sense?" If the passage doesn't make sense, encourage your child to reread the segment that needs clarification.

Directions: Read the passage and answer the following questions.

The Strange and Endangered Okapi

The okapi is a strange and unique animal. It is endangered, which means there are not many okapis left in the world. Nobody knew about the Okapi until scientists discovered it in the Congo rainforest of Africa in 1901. It looks like a horse or zebra, but it isn't related to either animal. The okapi is actually related to the giraffe. The okapi's neck is long. Its head is light in color with a pointed head and large erect ears, while its back legs and hind end have dark purplish stripes on its coat. Its strange color and its ability to stand perfectly still for over an hour help the okapi blend into the rainforest. Okapis eat grasses, leaves, and seeds. The okapi has a long tongue that it can extend to wash its own eyes. Male okapis have small horns, but unlike most mammals, the female is usually larger than the male of the species. Okapis can grow to be over five feet tall. The Okapi is a shy animal, so even if you go to the Congo, you might never see one.

1.   What is the main idea of this passage?

    a.   To describe the okapi
    b.   To tell why the okapi is an endangered animal
    c.   To understand how to protect an endangered animal
    d   To explain why the okapi is a mammal

2.   The word *unique* probably means

    a.   just like other animals
    b.   different
    c.   the same
    d.   endangered

3.   From this passage we know that the okapi uses its tongue to

        a.   clean its fur
        b.   wash its pointed ears
        c.   wash its eyes
        d.   drink water

4.   Which is not a reason why you might never see an okapi?

        a.   the okapi can stay perfectly still for over an hour
        b.   the okapi is a shy animal
        c.   the male is smaller than the female
        d.   the okapi's stripes help it blend in with the rain forest trees

5.   How are male and female okapis different?

        a.   males have a longer tongue
        b.   females are larger than males
        c.   males are lighter in color
        d.   females have purplish stripes

Read the passage and answer the following questions.

Surfing the Internet

The Internet users group is growing every day. People are finding more and more reasons to turn to the Internet. It doesn't matter how old you are, the Internet has something for you. Many adults use the Internet at their office, while others use it at home. Children can access the Internet from their home computer or even their school's computer.

There are many reasons why people access the Internet. One of the main reasons why people pay to become Internet users is to receive e-mail. E-mail is electronic mail. Another reason why people access the Internet is to "surf" the World Wide Web. The World Wide Web is made up of many web sites that people can go to in order to find out information on almost anything. When people visit different web sites, it's called "surfing."

How can you become an Internet user? Well, first you must have access to a computer and a telephone line. Then your parents need to sign up with an Internet service provider, which is sometimes called an I.S.P. With an I.S.P., you pay a monthly fee, and then no matter where you visit on the Internet, you don't have to pay for expensive long distance telephone calls. Finally, you need to get a web browser for your computer. Once you have these three things, you are ready to "surf" the Internet.

Although the Internet can be fun, it is definitely not a toy. Children and adults alike need to be responsible and safe when using the Internet. Children should always be careful to visit only the websites that their parents have approved, they should access the Internet with adult supervision, and they shouldn't give out their name or address to strangers on the Internet. If you are already an Internet user or if you plan to use the Internet soon, just remember to be responsible, be safe, and have fun!

1. In this passage, the word *access* probably means

    a. to ride
    b. to get onto
    c. to break in
    d. to look at

2. Which item is not always needed to access the Internet?

    a. a home computer
    b. an Internet service provider
    c. a web browser
    d. a telephone line

3.   Why do you think the Internet is not a toy?

     a.   because it can break
     b.   because you can't hold it in your hand
     c.   because strangers also use the Internet
     d.   because toys are only for children

4.   What would not be a good reason to access the Internet?

     a.   to surf the web
     b.   to get e-mail
     c.   to make long distance telephone calls
     d.   to look for information

5.   What is this passage mainly about?

     a.   accessing the Internet
     b.   how to surf the Internet
     c.   buying a home computer
     d.   Internet safety

Content Cluster: FUNCTIONAL READING

Objective: To evaluate reading comprehension skills using functional text.

Parent Tip: Functional reading is material read to perform a task. Encourage your child to read and follow directions such as recipes or board games. Ask simple questions like, "What do we do first?" As a comprehension check when your child finishes reading the directions.

Use the following recipe to answer the following questions.

Grammy's World's Greatest Chocolate Chip Cookies
Ingredients

2	cups flour	3/4	cup butter
1/2	tsp salt	5/8	cup sugar
1	tsp baking soda	5/8	cup brown sugar
1 1/2	tsp vanilla	1	egg
1	12 oz. package of semisweet chocolate chips		

Baking Instructions

Preheat oven to 350°. Mix sugar, brown sugar, butter, vanilla, and egg in large pan. Stir in flour, soda, and salt. Add chocolate chips. Place tablespoons of dough onto cookie sheet about 2 inches apart. Bake for 12-15 minutes on a cookie sheet.

1.   This recipe has instructions for making

    a.   eggs
    b.   chocolate chips
    c.   cookies
    d.   flour

2.   Which of these items is probably not needed to make this recipe?

    a.   a measuring cup
    b.   a cookie sheet
    c.   a spoon
    d.   a knife

3.   Which ingredient is the last one added to this recipe?

   a.   sugar
   b.   chocolate chips
   c.   egg
   d.   salt

4.   The term *place* in this recipe probably means

   a.   somewhere to go
   b.   a location
   c.   to set
   d.   to smash

5.   What might be the next step in this recipe?

   a.   eat the cookies
   b.   take the cookies out of the oven
   c.   turn off the oven
   d.   put the cookies in a cookie jar

Read the passage and answer the following questions.

How to Take a Test

There are very few people who like to take tests, so if you have to take a test, then follow these simple directions to help yourself do better on the test.

1.   The first thing you need to do is study. Find a quiet place, don't turn on the television or the radio, and sit at a desk or table to study, not the floor. You don't want to fall asleep while studying.

2.   It is also important to get a good night's sleep the night before the test. A good night's sleep helps you think clearly during the test.

3.   Make sure to eat a good meal before taking your test. A big meal might make you sleepy, so eat a light meal or a snack and you won't get hungry during the test.

4.   Right before you take the test, practice deep breathing. Taking deep breaths helps you get oxygen to your brain, helps you relax, and helps you have a clear head.

5.   Finally, during the test, don't spend too much time on one answer. If you get stuck on a problem, skip it and return to it later. Students often spend too much time on one problem and don't finish the test.

6.   Good luck with your test!

1.   What should you do while taking a test?

    a.   study
    b.   eat a snack
    c.   breathe deeply
    d.   don't spend too much time on one answer

2.   In this passage, the word *light* means ...

    a.   not heavy
    b.   full of sunshine
    c.   tasty
    d.   good

3.   According to the directions, why should you get a good night's sleep?

    a.   it gets oxygen to your brain
    b.   it helps you think clearly
    c.   it makes you sleepy
    d.   it helps you relax

4.   What is the main idea of this passage?

    a.   how to avoid falling asleep
    b.   how to study for a test
    c.   how to take a test
    d.   how to eat right

5.   What is the last instruction for taking a test?

    a.   eat a snack
    b.   have fun
    c.   get a good night's sleep
    d.   skip an answer if you get stuck

LANGUAGE

Content Cluster: MECHANICS

Subcluster: CAPITALIZATION

Objective: To evaluate the correct use of capitalization.

> **Parent Tip:** Help your child learn about correct capitalization and punctuation by reinforcing rules as you read all types of materials with your child. Take note of punctuation in newspapers, stories, business letters, and textbooks, and point them out. Make sure your child knows to capitalize proper nouns and the beginning word of a sentence.

Mark the answer that shows the correct capitalization.

Example: We have a test this <u>friday evening</u>.

    a.   Friday evening
    b.   Friday Evening
    c.   friday Evening
    d.   Correct as is

The correct answer is "a". Only Friday needs to be capitalized.

1.   My favorite team played in the <u>Super bowl</u> last year.

    a.   super bowl
    b.   Super Bowl
    c.   super Bowl
    d.   Correct as is

2.   In third grade we will learn about <u>Native Americans</u>.

    a.   native americans
    b.   Native americans
    c.   native americans
    d.   Correct as is

3.   The car stopped at <u>North Kennedy avenue</u>.

    a.   north Kennedy avenue
    b.   North Kennedy Avenue
    c.   north kennedy avenue
    d.   Correct as is

4.   Did you ever read <u>the lion, the witch, and the wardrobe</u>?

    a.   The Lion, The Witch, And The Wardrobe
    b.   The Lion, the witch, and the wardrobe
    c.   The Lion, the Witch, and the Wardrobe
    d.   Correct as is

5.   We had no school on <u>president's day</u>.

    a.   President's Day
    b.   President's day
    c.   president's day
    d.   Correct as is

Content Cluster: MECHANICS

Subcluster: PUNCTUATION

Objective: To evaluate the correct use of punctuation.

Parent Tip: To encourage correct punctuation in your child's writing, have him/her correct his/her own writing by playing red light/green light. Ask your child to trace the capital letter at the beginning of each sentence with a green pen and trace the sentence-ending punctuation with a red pen.

Mark the answer that shows the correct punctuation.

Example: Jeremy didnt go to the movies.

    a.   did'nt
    b.   didn't
    c.   didnt'
    d.   Correct as is

The correct answer is "b". Didn't is the contraction for did not. The apostrophe replaces the "o" and is inserted between the "n" and "t".

1.   Where does your grandmother live

    a.   .
    b.   !
    c.   ?
    d.   Correct as is

2.   What a beautiful day?

    a.   !
    b.   .
    c.   ,
    d.   Correct as is

3.   Her birthday party was on Sunday, December 13, 1998.

    a.   Sunday December 13, 1998
    b.   Sunday December 13 1998
    c.   Sunday, December 13 1998
    d.   Correct as is

Use Shawn's letter to answer questions 4 and 5.

September 14, 1997

(4) Dear Jamal

I can't wait to visit you this summer in New York. We are going to have a great time!

(5) Sincerely
Shawn

4. a. dear jamal
    b. Dear jamal,
    c. Dear Jamal,
    d. Correct as is

5. a. sincerely,
    b. Sincerely,
    c. Sincerely
    d. Correct as is

Content Cluster: MECHANICS

Subcluster: USAGE

Objective: To evaluate the correct use of noun-verb agreement.

Parent Tip: Verb tense and noun-verb agreements are important aspects of grammar usage. Help your child use noun-verb agreement correctly in writing and speaking by correcting grammatical errors as they occur. You can practice this with your child by using the incorrect noun-verb combination and having your child correct you.

Directions: Choose the correct word or words to replace the incorrect underlined word or words in the sentence. If the sentence is already correct, choose "Correct as is".

Example: Rick and Jenna <u>enjoys</u> going to the movies.

    a.   enjoying
    b.   have enjoys
    c.   have enjoy
    d.   enjoy

The correct answer is "d". The verb enjoy is the best answer.

1.   Luci <u>thinked</u> about last year's summer vacation.

    a.   have thinked
    b.   think
    c.   thought
    d.   Correct as is

2.   The <u>three girls sings</u> well together.

    a.   three girl sings
    b.   three girl sing
    c.   three girls sing
    d.   Correct as is

3. The astronauts <u>will goes</u> to the moon.

    a. will go
    b. wills go
    c. wills goes
    d. Correct as is

4. My aquarium <u>has four fishes</u> in the water.

    a. have four fishes
    b. has four fish
    c. have four fish
    d. Correct as is

5. <u>Lance and Mina playing</u> together every day.

    a. Lance and Mina is playing
    b. Lance and Mina plays
    c. Lance and Mina play
    d. Correct as is

Content Cluster: EXPRESSION

Subcluster: SENTENCE STRUCTURE

Objective: To evaluate knowledge of correct sentence structure.

Parent Tip: Your child should be able to combine sentences using commas and conjunctions, or recognize an incomplete sentence. Children at this stage of development tend to overuse "and" as well as run-on sentences. Help your child become a stronger writer by creating shorter sentences and using more punctuation.

Directions: Choose the sentence that is written correctly. If the sentence is already correct, choose "Correct as is".

Example: Nick will sell his skateboard. And will sell his rollerblades.

    a.   Nick will sell. His skateboard and his rollerblades.
    b.   Nick will sell his skateboard. And his rollerblades.
    c.   Nick will sell his skateboard and his rollerblades.
    d.   Nick will sell his skateboard, and his rollerblades.

The correct answer is "c".

1.   Jason ate his pizza, he drank his milk.

    a.   Jason ate his pizza, and he drank his milk.
    b.   Jason ate his pizza and he drank his milk.
    c.   Jason ate his pizza he drank his milk.
    d.   Correct as is

2.   Grandma, walking slowly, she answered the door.

    a.   Grandma was walking slowly, answered the door.
    b.   Grandma was walking slowly she answered the door.
    c.   Grandma, walking slowly, answered the door.
    d.   Correct as is

3.   The baby cried. Loudly until she fell asleep.

    a.   The baby cried loudly until she fell asleep.
    b.   The baby cried loudly, until she fell asleep.
    c.   The baby cried loudly. Until she fell asleep.
    d.   Correct as is

4.   Eating ice cream. At the ballgame is fun.

    a.   Eating ice cream at the ballgame. Is fun.
    b.   Eating ice cream at the ballgame is fun.
    c.   Eating ice cream, at the ballgame, is fun.
    d.   Correct as is

5.   Bananas grow in tropical climates, and are usually yellow.

    a.   Bananas growing in tropical climates and are usually yellow.
    b.   Bananas grows in tropical climates and are usually yellow.
    c.   Bananas grow in tropical climates and are usually yellow.
    d.   Correct as is.

Content Cluster: EXPRESSION

Subcluster: CONTENT AND ORGANIZATION

Objective: To evaluate knowledge of an organized and well-written passage.

Parent Tip: It is important for your child to write a coherent paragraph. His/her thoughts need to be organized and focused. Have your child keep a writing journal in which s/he writes often. Select topics for him/her to write about which are relevant to his/her life, fun, and exciting. Always go over their writing with them to see if their writing is focused and organized. Good writers often organize their thoughts in an outline or a web before they actually write.

Directions: Use the paragraph below to answer the questions.

My Best Friend

My best friend in the world is Gina. Gina and I do many fun things together. We go to Brownies and soccer practice every week. Sometimes we pretend we are famous movie stars, and other times we play in my tree house. Marika is in my art class. Gina and I even have the same teacher.

1.   Which of these sentences does not belong in the paragraph?

    a.   Gina and I do many fun things together.
    b.   We go to Brownies and soccer practice every week.
    c.   Marika is in my art class.
    d.   Gina and I even have the same teacher.

2.   Which sentence would not belong in this paragraph.

    a.   Gina and I watch television together.
    b.   Gina's mom likes chocolate cake.
    c.   Gina and I go to the same school.
    d.   Gina and I pretend to wear make-up.

3.   What is the topic sentence of this paragraph?

      a.   Gina and I do many fun things together.
      b.   Gina and I even have the same teacher.
      c.   We go to Brownies and soccer practice every week.
      d.   My best friend in the world is Gina.

4.   What would be a good closing sentence for this paragraph?

      a.   Gina and I will probably be best friends forever.
      b.   Gina lives two houses away from me.
      c.   Gina's mom helps her do her homework.
      d.   Gina and I wear the same tennis shoes.

5.   What is the main idea of this paragraph?

      a.   To tell about soccer practice.
      b.   To tell why Gina is the author's best friend.
      c.   To describe Gina.
      d.   To tell what Gina likes to do.

Content Cluster: STUDY SKILLS

Subcluster: DICTIONARY SKILLS

Objective: To evaluate knowledge of dictionary use to identify word meaning.

Parent Tip: Your third grader should know how to use a dictionary. S/he should be familiar with guidewords, know that words are arranged alphabetically, know how to use the pronunciation key, and realize that there are often multiple meanings for one word. Keep a dictionary available for your child to use. Encourage him/her to look up words frequently to acquire these skills. Have your child select an unknown word daily, determine it's meaning, and reward him/her for using it throughout the day.

Directions: Use these guidewords from a dictionary page to answer questions 1 and 2.

Example: Which word would not be found on the dictionary page?

Life – love

    a. live
    b. long
    c. look
    d. lovely

The correct answer is "d". Lovely would not be on the page.

1. Which word would not be found on the dictionary page?

    a. sail   **safe - secret**
    b. send
    c. scared
    d. second

2. Which word would not be found on the dictionary page?

   a. garlic   **garden - goal**
   b. goat
   c. general
   d. glad

3. Which word has the same sound as the "oo" in root?

   a. book
   b. fruit
   c. hood
   d. storm

4. Which word has the same sound as the "mb" in remember?

   a. bomber
   b. tomb
   c. comb
   d. slumber

5. The word <u>real</u> sounds most like the word

   a. kneel
   b. dead
   c. healthy
   d. lend

Content Cluster: STUDY SKILLS

Subcluster: GENERAL REFERENCE SOURCES

Objective: To evaluate the correct use of reference sources and materials.

Parent Tip: Any kind of reading is important. Help your child become familiar with a dictionary, thesaurus, encyclopedia, atlas, and even the table of contents in a book. Encourage your child to use these resources whenever possible. Use your child's imagination as you take pretend trips around the world together. Use the reference materials as a resource to learn about these new and exciting places.

Directions: Choose the best answer to each of the following questions.

Example: Which of the following would you most likely find at the beginning of a chapter book?

  a. dictionary
  b. table of contents
  c. thesaurus
  d. atlas

The correct answer is "b". A table of contents is located at the beginning of a book.

1. To find out about today's weather you should look in a(n)

  a. dictionary
  b. newspaper
  c. thesaurus
  d. encyclopedia

2. To look up the definition of the word "thunder" you should look in a(n)

  a. dictionary
  b. newspaper
  c. atlas
  d. encyclopedia

3. To find a synonym for the word "smooth", you should look in a(n)

    a. dictionary
    b. table of contents
    c. thesaurus
    d. atlas

4. To look at a map of the United States, you should look at a(n)

    a. newspaper
    b. atlas
    c. table of contents
    d. encyclopedia

5. Where might you look to do research for a report on the United States?

    a. dictionary
    b. thesaurus
    c. encyclopedia
    d. atlas

SPELLING

Content Cluster: CONTENT

Subcluster: SIGHT WORDS

Objective: To evaluate recognition of misspelled words by sight.

Parent Tip: Your child needs to be able to recognize both correctly and incorrectly spelled words. As you read with your child, pay particular attention to words that don't follow the "rules". For example, if your child comes across the word *heading*, you might see if your child recognizes that "ea" normally expresses a long e sound. Make a word wall in your child's bedroom where s/he can post any words that don't follow the rules. S/he will eventually learn to recognize and spell them correctly.

Directions: Mark the sentence that has a misspelled word in it. If no words are misspelled, mark the answer "No mistake."

Example:

    a. The queen had a <u>jewel</u> on her crown.
    b. What is your favorite animal in the <u>ocean</u>?
    c. Frank got into a <u>fight</u> at school.
    d. No mistake

The correct answer is "d". All three sentences are correct.

1. a. Lucy ate her <u>soup</u> with a spoon.
   b. I <u>allmost</u> missed the bus this morning.
   c. Mark had a scary <u>dream</u> last night.
   d. No mistake

2. a. We flew in a <u>large</u> airplane.
   b. I <u>know</u> a secret.
   c. Suzanne needed a <u>light</u> to see in the dark.
   d. No mistake

3. a. Joanne marked the <u>rong</u> answer.
    b. <u>Bring</u> a dollar for the arcade.
    c. She bumped her <u>head</u> on the car door.
    d. No mistake

4. a. We <u>walk</u> to school every day.
    b. My <u>father</u> is my hero.
    c. I <u>nead</u> a pencil for the test.
    d. No mistake

5. a. I love my mom <u>because</u> she helps me.
    b. <u>Were</u> are you going?
    c. The elephant's <u>trunk</u> sprays water.
    d. No mistake

Content Cluster: PHONETIC PRINCIPLES

Subcluster: CONSONANT SOUNDS

Objective: To evaluate recognition and application of consonants and consonant clusters.

Parent Tip: Spelling is a difficult task for most students. It is therefore helpful when a child is able to recognize words or word chunks (such as "ing") within a word. Building upon this skill will assist your child in both reading and spelling.

Directions: Mark the sentence that has a misspelled word in it. If no words are misspelled, mark the answer "No mistake."

Example:

    a.   The policeman showed us his <u>badge</u>.
    b.   Mom gets up at the crack of <u>dawn</u> every day.
    c.   The mouse <u>skurried</u> into its hole.
    d.   No mistake

The correct answer is "c". The correct spelling is scurried.

1.   a.   It <u>sure</u> is a beautiful day today!
    b.   How many minutes <u>untill</u> recess?
    c.   Grandma makes the best <u>fudge</u> ever!
    d.   No mistake

2.   a.   Did you really see a <u>gost</u>?
    b.   Joey had an <u>ache</u> in his leg.
    c.   He fed his bunny a <u>carrot</u>.
    d.   No mistake

3. a. The <u>dolphin</u> swam in the water.
    b. Dad will <u>scold</u> you if you tell a lie.
    c. She blew the <u>whissle</u> at the end of recess.
    d. No mistake

4. a. His skin felt dry and <u>rough</u>.
    b. She heard the <u>telefone</u> ring.
    c. All of her friends moved away <u>except</u> Tina.
    d. No mistake

5. a. Mom bought a <u>gallon</u> of milk.
    b. We split the pizza in <u>half</u>.
    c. She spent fifty <u>cens</u> on her soda.
    d. No mistake

Content Cluster: PHONETIC PRINCIPLES
Subcluster: VOWEL SOUNDS

Objective: To evaluate knowledge of vowel and vowel cluster recognition.

Parent Tip: When two vowels go walking, the first one does the talking. This rule is important to remember for beginning readers, but the reality is that there are more exceptions to this rule than words that follow the rule. Therefore, it is important that we check the word after we spell it. After your child spells the word, ask them if the word follows a rule or is an exception to that rule.

Directions: Mark the sentence that has a misspelled word in it. If no words are misspelled, mark the answer "No mistake."

Example:
    a.   The <u>wayter</u> brought us our meal.
    b.   You can <u>build</u> anything with blocks and your imagination.
    c.   She <u>said</u> that she didn't like the movie.
    d.   No mistake

The correct answer is "a". The correct spelling is waiter.

1.
    a.   One <u>monkey</u> jumped from tree to tree.
    b.   The box is too <u>heavey</u> to lift.
    c.   People wear hats to <u>cover</u> their heads.
    d.   No mistake

2.
    a.   A lake can <u>freeze</u> in the winter.
    b.   George went to the <u>docter</u> when he hurt his foot.
    c.   How do you like your <u>steak</u> cooked?
    d.   No mistake

3.
    a.   You should eat <u>salad</u> for dinner.
    b.   Can you turn some <u>music</u> on the radio?
    c.   I hope I can solve your <u>problum</u>.
    d.   No mistake

4.
    a.   Please read <u>chapter</u> two for homework.
    b.   She put the <u>blankit</u> on her bed.
    c.   How many people are in your <u>family</u>?
    d.   No mistake

5.
    a.   Move <u>forword</u> five yellow spaces.
    b.   The Three Billy <u>Goats</u> Gruff is a great story.
    c.   Our <u>earth</u> is the third planet from the sun.
    d.   No mistake

Content Cluster: STRUCTURAL PRINCIPLES
Subcluster: INFLECTIONAL ENDINGS

Objective: To evaluate recognition and application of word endings.

Parent Tip: When we think of spelling we usually look for spelling rules to assist us. While there are only a few rules to help us with word endings, they prove very useful. 1. Change "y" to "i" and add "ed" or "es." 2. When adding "ing" drop the "e." 3. The "shun" sound is usually spelled "tion."

Directions: Mark the sentence that has a misspelled word in it. If no words are misspelled, mark the answer "No mistake."

Example:
   a.   The <u>eagle</u> soared over the mountain.
   b.   We are studying <u>geometree</u> in math.
   c.   My favorite color is <u>purple</u>.
   d.   No mistake

The correct answer is "b". The correct spelling is geometry.

1.   a.   She broke her <u>ankle</u> in the race.
      b.   Can you <u>draw</u> a picture?
      c.   Laura <u>closd</u> the door to her house.
      d.   No mistake

2.   a.   Stephan found five <u>pennys</u> in his pocket.
      b.   The <u>crowd</u> cheered at the ballgame.
      c.   We all want to be <u>first</u> in line.
      d.   No mistake

3.   a.   David is <u>moveing</u> to a new school.
      b.   The southeast <u>region</u> of the United States has lots of rain.
      c.   Have you <u>given</u> any money to the poor?
      d.   No mistake

4.   a.   The bowling ball <u>rolled</u> toward the pins.
      b.   I smell a funny <u>oder</u> in the air.
      c.   The gum costs a <u>nickel</u>.
      d.   No mistake

5.   a.   You put <u>lotion</u> on dry skin.
      b.   Josh <u>grew</u> up in a small town.
      c.   Are you <u>readey</u> to go to lunch?
      d.   No mistake

Content Cluster: STRUCTURAL PRINCIPLES
Subcluster: AFFIXES

Objective: To evaluate knowledge of recognition and application of suffixes and prefixes.

> **Parent Tip:** Help your child to become familiar with common prefixes and suffixes that will help him/her analyze a word and determine its meaning from its parts. As students associate meaning to parts of words they know, they are better able to evaluate new words in reading. When students begin to recognize these affixes, they will also begin to recognize familiar root words. This is important, as it may determine the meaning of the entire word.

Prefixes and their meanings:	Suffixes and their meanings:
re = to do again or from	er = one who does
un = not	ful = full of
equa = like or same	able = able to
dis = not	ship = the condition of
de = separate	ly = in the manner of
mis = not or wrongly	tion = the state of
pre = before	less = without

Directions: Mark the sentence that has a misspelled word in it. If no words are misspelled, mark the answer "No mistake."

Example:

    a.   She stuck her tongue out <u>rudely</u> at her teacher.
    b.   The <u>laboror</u> worked in the fields.
    c.   He was a <u>fearless</u> firefighter.
    d.   No mistake

The correct answer is "b". The correct spelling is laborer.

1.   a.   I am <u>thankful</u> for my friends.
       b.   Will you <u>refill</u> my soda?
       c.   A chameleon can become <u>innvisible</u> to its predators.
       d.   No mistake

2.   a.   I hope you don't <u>misslead</u> your little sister.
       b.   You should be <u>careful</u> crossing the street.
       c.   The plane ride made her stomach feel <u>uneasy</u>.
       d.   No mistake

3. a. We had a <u>wonderfull</u> time at the amusement park!
    b. Jonah had to <u>retake</u> his school picture.
    c. Luci was filled with <u>sadness</u> as she said goodbye.
    d. No mistake

4. a. "I will be back <u>shortly</u>," said Dad.
    b. Don was a <u>helpful</u> student in class.
    c. Jordan knew the trip to the store was <u>unecessary</u>.
    d. No mistake

5. a. Two families had an <u>enjoyable</u> time at the picnic.
    b. Dinah <u>worked</u> hard on her school report.
    c. The judge had to <u>dismiss</u> the charges against the criminal.
    d. No mistake

Content Cluster: STRUCTURAL PRINCIPLES
Subcluster: HOMOPHONES

Objective: To evaluate recognition and selection of the appropriate homophone in a sentence.

Parent Tip: Homophones have the same sound but are spelled differently. Therefore it is important that children are able to see the word along with hearing it. This will help them remember which homophone to select.

Directions: Mark the sentence that has a misspelled word in it. If no words are misspelled, mark the answer "No mistake."

Example: a.   The balloon went <u>hire</u> into the air.
           b.   She seasoned her spaghetti sauce with <u>thyme</u>.
           c.   The criminal had to <u>flee</u> the country.
           d.   No mistake
The correct answer is "a". The correct spelling is higher.

1.   a.   She put one cup of <u>flower</u> in the cake.
     b.   What shirt should I <u>wear</u> today?
     c.   Karl tried not to <u>stare</u> at the lady's dress.
     d.   No mistake

2.   a.   We elect a <u>new</u> president every four years.
     b.   What will you <u>buy</u> with your money?
     c.   Mom put a <u>pair</u> in my lunch.
     d.   No mistake

3.   a.   Do you <u>know</u> the right answer?
     b.   We ate a <u>stake</u> for dinner.
     c.   She wore a <u>blue</u> dress.
     d.   No mistake

4.   a.   My grandpa was a <u>grate</u> man.
     b.   Rose had a <u>seam</u> on her skirt.
     c.   Your story doesn't make <u>sense</u>.
     d.   No mistake

5.   a.   The black <u>knight</u> will joust with the white knight.
     b.   There was <u>do</u> on the grass in the morning.
     c.   The students need a <u>break</u> during the test.
     d.   No mistake

ANSWER KEY

Reading Vocabulary

Synonyms
1. c
2. d
3. c
4. c
5. b

Multiple Meanings
1. b
2. d
3. a
4. d
5. d

Context
1. c
2. b
3. d
4. c
5. b

Reading Comprehension

Recreational
1. b
2. c
3. d
4. a
5. c
1. c
2. b
3. d
4. b
5. c

Textual
1. a
2. b
3. c

4. c
5. b
1. b
2. a
3. c
4. c
5. a

Functional
1. c
2. d
3. b
4. c
5. b
1. d
2. a
3. b
4. c
5. d

Language

Mechanics
1. b
2. d
3. b
4. c
5. a

Punctuation
1. c
2. a
3. d
4. c
5. b

Usage
1. c
2. c
3. a
4. b
5. c

Expression

Sentence Structure
1. a
2. c
3. a
4. b
5. c

Content and Organization
1. c
2. b
3. d
4. a
5. b

Study Skills

Dictionary Skills
1. b
2. b
3. b
4. d
5. a

General Reference Sources
1. b
2. a
3. c
4. b
5. c

Spelling

Sight Words
1. b
2. d
3. a
4. c
5. b

Phonetic Principles

Consonant Sounds
1. b
2. a
3. c
4. b
5. c

Vowel Sounds
1. b
2. b
3. c
4. b
5. a

Structural Principals

Inflectional Endings
1. c
2. a
3. a
4. b
5. c

Affixes
1. c
2. a
3. a
4. c
5. c

Homophones
1. a
2. c
3. b
4. a
5. b

MATHEMATICS: PROBLEM SOLVING

Content Cluster: CONCEPTS OF WHOLE NUMBER COMPUTATION

Objective: To evaluate comprehension of whole numbers when displayed in various formats.

Parent Tip: It is important for your child to understand the meaning of numbers and concepts such as multiplication. To ensure that your child understands these concepts, encourage him/her to write simple equations like 2 x 5 = 10, so they are not in such familiar forms. Another way to write this could be 10 = 2 x 5. You might even ask your child to write a number like 5 in as many different ways as possible. Some answers might include roman numeral V, 4 + 1, etc. The goal is for your child to understand numbers beyond the memorization of facts.

Directions: Read the problem and choose the best answer.

Example: What is another way to write 3 x 7 = 21

     a.   21 x 7 = 3
     b.   21 = 7 x 3
     c.   3 ÷ 7 = 21
     d.   7 ÷ 3 = 21

The correct answer is "b". 21 = 7 x 3 is the same as 3 x 7 = 21

1.   Which has the same value as 12 x 4?

     a.   4 + 4 + 4 + 4
     b.   12 + 12 + 12 + 12
     c.   4 ÷ 12
     d.   12 ÷ 4

2.   Which is another way to write 7 + 7 + 7?

     a.   7 x 7 x 7
     b.   7 ÷ 3
     c.   7 x 3
     d.   7 + 3

3.   Which is another way to write 426?

    a.   4,000 + 20 + 6
    b.   400 + 20 + 6
    c.   40 + 20 + 6
    d.   600 + 20 + 4

4.   Which of the numbers has a 6 in the 10's place?

    a.   1,161
    b.   1,116
    c.   1,611
    d.   6,116

5.   Which group of numbers has the most odd numbers?

    a.   17, 36, 49, 53, 62, 85
    b.   16, 27, 38, 56, 92, 83
    c.   43, 27, 15, 72, 88, 64
    d.   24, 68, 93, 44, 80, 76

Content Cluster: NUMBER SENSE AND NUMERATION

Objective: To evaluate number sense, order, and place value.

Parent Tip: A child often arrives at an obviously erroneous answer to a math problem. S/he might say $10 \div 5 = 50$. Have your child get into the habit of checking an answer to see if it makes sense. Help to make the problem more concrete. For example, you might ask whether 10 cookies divided by 5 people could give each person 50 cookies. Eventually your child will develop the habit of checking his/her answer and will catch his/her own mistakes.

Directions: Read the problem and choose the best answer.

Example: Rex scored an even number of baskets in his basketball game. How many points did he score?

    a.   23
    b.   19
    c.   16
    d.   21

The correct answer is "c". The even number is 16.

1.   How many of these numbers are greater than 215?
        224, 426, 512, 152, 207

    a.   5
    b.   2
    c.   3
    d.   4

2.   If Jerry is 10th in the lunch line, how many people are ahead of him?

    a.   10
    b.   11
    c.   9
    d.   1

3.   Which number is 10 less than 4,762?

  a. 3,762
  b. 4,662
  c. 4,752
  d. 4,862

4.   How many thousands are in 3,605?

  a. five
  b. six
  c. zero
  d. three

5.   What is another way to say 9 hundreds, 3 ones, 2 thousands, 8 tens, and 6 ten-thousands?

  a. 93,286
  b. 62,983
  c. 38,926
  d. 983,620

Content Cluster: GEOMETRY AND SPATIAL SENSE

Objective: To evaluate understanding of geometric shapes and spatial ability.

Parent Tip: Children need to be able to recognize geometrical shapes by third grade. There are shapes all around us in our everyday lives. A cereal box is a rectangular prism, and a basketball is a sphere. You might ask your child what shape a stop sign represents, or you might see the Pentagon in Washington D.C on television, and point out that the building has five sides. Use these moments to reinforce the math your child is learning at school.

Read the problem and choose the best answer.

Example: Which shape is a pentagon?

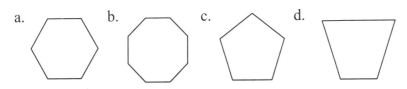

a.   b.   c.   d.

The correct answer is "c". A pentagon has 5 sides and angles.

1.   Which figure is the same size and shape as the sample?

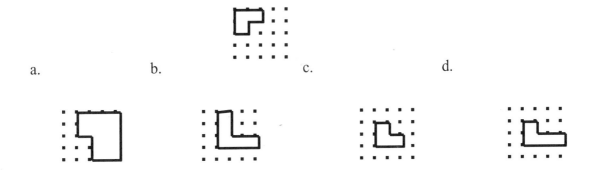

    a.   b.   c.   d.

2.   Which of these letters can be folded in half so the parts match exactly?

    a. **T**   b. **L**   c. **G**   d. **J**

3.   Which shows the location of the earth?

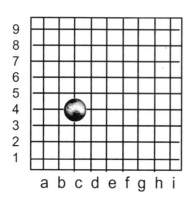

a.   c5
b.   c4
c.   c3
d.   d4

4.   Which shape comes on the right of the largest triangle?

a.   the smallest triangle
b.   the smallest circle
c.   the medium circle
d.   the medium triangle

5.   How many more of the small diamonds would it take to fill the large diamond?

a.   3
b.   9
c.   6
d.   7

Content Cluster: MEASUREMENT

Objective: To evaluate standard and metric units of measurement, date, time, and money usage.

Parent Tip: Children in the third grade must be able to tell time, measure perimeter and area, and use both the metric and U.S. customary forms of measurement like meters and centimeters or inches and yards. Help your children by showing them that there are weight measurements on cans, cartons, and boxes. You could challenge them to find ten items in the kitchen that are measured in liters, or five items that could be measured in inches or centimeters.

Read the problem and choose the best answer.

Example: Which angle is greater than a right angle.

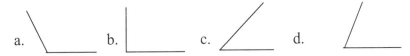

The correct answer is "a". Choice b is a right angle, and c and d are smaller than a right angle.

1. What would you use to measure the length of the school playground?

    a.   yards
    b.   millimeters
    c.   inches
    d.   miles

2. What could be the temperature on a hot summer day?

    a.   55°F
    b.   23°F
    c.   85°F
    d.   70°F

3. Steve bought an apple for $0.25 and an orange for $0.30. If he gave the cashier $1.00, how much change should he receive?

    a. $0.55
    b. $0.70
    c. $0.75
    d. $0.45

4.   What day is the third Sunday of December?

December

Sunday	Monday	Tuesday	Wednesday	Thursday	Friday	Saturday
	1	2	3	4	5	6
7	8	9	10	11	12	13
14	15	16	17	18	19	20
21	22	23	24	25	26	27
28	29	30	31			

    a.   December 14
    b.   December 27
    c.   December 20
    d.   December 21

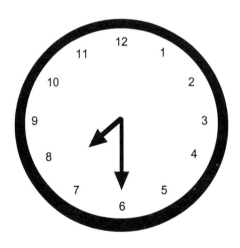

5.   What time is not displayed on the clock?

    a.   half-past seven
    b.   six thirty-seven
    c.   seven thirty
    d.   thirty minutes before eight

Content Cluster: STATISTICS AND PROBABILITY

Objective: To evaluate prediction skills and the students' ability to read and interpret graphs.

Parent Tip: To understand statistics on an elementary level, your child needs to be able to make a prediction as to the outcome of a certain event. Children are often reluctant to guess at an answer. For example, if a coin is flipped, will it come up heads or tails? Prediction is also a skill that your child can develop while reading. As you are reading together, stop and ask what might happen next. Statistics also involves graphing. Expose your child to different types of graphs that you might encounter in magazines or newspapers. Bar graphs, line graphs, tally graphs, and pie charts are some examples of graphs with which your child should be familiar.

Read the problem and choose the best answer.

Example: If a quarter is flipped 10 times, how many times will it probably be heads?

     a.   0
     b.   5
     c.   10
     d.   8

The correct answer is "b". There are two sides on a coin, so it will land on heads about half the time.

1.   If Jack takes one jelly bean, which color will he most likely get?

     a.   red
     b.   blue
     c.   yellow
     d.   All the same

50 red
30 blue
20 yellow

Use the following information to answer questions 2 and 3.

2.   Who read the least amount of books in June?

Books Read in June

a.	Juan		Juan	5
b.	Julie		Julie	10
c.	Sam		Sam	6
d.	Nina		Nina	9

3.   How many more books did Nina read than Juan?

    a.   14
    b.   9
    c.   4
    d.   5

Use the graph to answer questions 4 and 5.

Food	# of Students
Hamburgers	5
Hot Dogs	6
Tacos	3
Pizza	8

4.   Which food did most students prefer?

    a.   hamburger
    b.   hot dog
    c.   taco
    d.   pizza

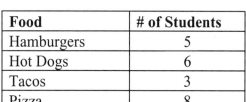

5.   Which was the second least popular food?

    a.   hamburger
    b.   hot dog
    c.   taco
    d.   pizza

Content Cluster: FRACTION AND DECIMAL CONCEPTS

Objective: To evaluate numerical and pictorial knowledge of fractions and decimals.

Parent Tip: Your child must not only recognize fractions and decimals in numeric and pictorial form, but s/he must also see how the two are related. For example, 2/10 equals .2 which also equals 1/5. Help your child recognize the fractions in real life experiences. You might ask what fraction of the family are girls, or what fraction of a pizza they just ate.

Read the problem and choose the best answer.

Example: What fraction of the squirrels are not black?

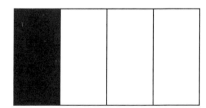

    a.   3/5
    b.   2/3
    c.   2/5
    d.   2/6

The correct answer is "c". The important word to notice is "not". Two out of five squirrels are "not" black.

1.   Which of the fractions is the same as the picture?

    a.   1/2
    b.   2/2
    c.   2/5
    d.   2/1

2.   What fraction of the model is shaded?

    a.   2/6
    b.   8/2
    c.   6/8
    d.   1/4

3.   Which decimal is the same as 2/10?

    a.   .2
    b.   2.0
    c.   .02
    d.   .002

4.   Looking at the diagram, what fraction means the same as

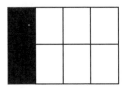

a.   b.    c.   d.

5.   Which picture is divided into equal pieces?

a. 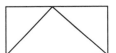   b.    c.    d.

Content Cluster: PATTERNS AND RELATIONSHIPS

Objective: To evaluate the ability to recognize patterns and relationships in numbers.

Parent Tip: Your child should be able to recognize patterns in numbers or the order in which things appear, and predict the number or item that might come next. Prediction is also a skill that your child can develop while reading. As you are reading together, stop and ask what might happen next. When your child is predicting a pattern, encourage him/her to draw a picture of the existing pattern or say it out loud. This may help your child predict what comes next in the pattern.

Read the problem and choose the best answer.

Example: What two coins complete the pattern?

    a.   a penny and a dime
    b.   a dime and a penny
    c.   two pennies
    d.   two dimes

The correct answer is "c". Two pennies follow each dime.

1.   What number comes next on the number line?

    a.   18
    b.   15
    c.   16
    d.   13

2.   Which pattern comes next?

                    *   **   ****   _____

    a.   *******
    b.   ******
    c.   **
    d.   *

3.   Which pattern comes next?

a.   b.   c.   d.

4.   What number comes next?

        1,001   2,003   3,005   _____

        a. 3,006
        b. 3,007
        c. 4,006
        d. 4,007

5.   What number best completes this equation?

        4 + 3 + 5 = 4 + _____

        a. 8
        b. 7
        c. 5
        d. 4

Content Cluster: ESTIMATION

Objective: *To evaluate knowledge of estimating or approximating numbers.*

Parent Tip: There are many times when an exact answer is not required. For example, if you were to give your child $10 to spend at the bookstore, and tell him/her that as s/he selects books to keep a running estimate, s/he will approximate when s/he might run out of money. Such tasks do not require exact answers, only approximations. Estimation is a simple skill to learn, and is one which people will use throughout their adult lives.

Directions: Read the problem and choose the best answer.

Example: Jimmy needed to buy parts to repair his bicycle. If he needed a chain for $2.75, a tire for $3.45, and a seat for $9.80, what is a fair estimate of his bill?

    a. $16
    b. $14
    c. $15
    d. $17

The correct answer is "a". The estimate would be $16.

1.   Nick bought the school supplies his teacher required. Approximately how much money did he spend?

School Supplies
Pencils $1.99
Notebooks $3.49
Markers $4.89
Folders $6.29

    a. $17
    b. $16
    c. $20
    d. $15

2.   Julia had $10 to spend at the toy store. Estimate how much change she should get if she bought a stuffed animal for $4.50 and a pack of stickers for $0.75.

    a. $5
    b. $4
    c. $6
    d. $0.40

3.   About how many blocks are in this cube?

     a.   7
     b.   12
     c.   1
     d.   8

4.   On her family's vacation, Yumi kept a record of how far her family traveled each day. Using the chart, estimate how far her family traveled altogether.

Day	Monday	Tuesday	Wednesday	Thursday	Friday
Miles	25	17	33	26	14

     a.   150 miles
     b.   130 miles
     c.   90 miles
     d.   120 miles

5.   Which answer is closest to 236?

     a.   23
     b.   240
     c.   37
     d.   230

MATHEMATICS: PROCEDURES

Content Cluster: NUMBER FACTS

Subcluster: MULTIPLICATION FACTS

Objective: To evaluate knowledge of multiplication facts 1 x 1 to 10 x 12.

Parent Tip: Third grade students must memorize their multiplication facts for numbers 1 to 10. Flashcards are very useful, as they can be practiced frequently. Once your children memorize these multiplication facts, it is important that they continue to practice them, or the facts quickly will be forgotten. Multiplication facts mean practice, practice, and continue to practice! Memorizing multiplication facts from 1 to 10 can be overwhelming for many students. Before they begin this task, make sure they understand the property of multiplication. (2 x 3 = 6 and 3 x 2 = 6). Once this is done, you can ease the memorization task by eliminating the redundant facts (i.e., there is no need to memorize 3 x 2 = 6 if 2 x 3 = 6 is already memorized.) The number of facts to memorize will drop from 108 to 72.

Directions: Read the problem and choose the best answer. If the answer is not given, choose answer "NH".

Example: 9 x 0 =

    a.   9
    b.   0
    c.   1
    d.   NH

The correct answer is "b". Any number multiplied by 0 is 0.

1.   5 x 3 =

    a.   8
    b.   15
    c.   5
    d.   NH

2.   12 x 11 =

    a.   122
    b.   121
    c.   132
    d.   NH

3.   7 x 0 =

    a.   7
    b.   1
    c.   0
    d.   NH

4.   7 x 8 =

    a.   15
    b.   65
    c.   55
    d.   NH

5.   9 x ___ = 72

    a.   9
    b.   7
    c.   8
    d.   NH

Content Cluster: NUMBER FACTS

Subcluster: DIVISION FACTS

Objective: To evaluate multiplication facts when presented in division form.

Parent Tip: Simple division facts are the inverse of multiplication facts. Many education stores now carry fact triangle flash cards that have both the multiplication and division relationships on them. It is important to use multiplication facts to check the answer to division problems, and vice versa. For example, if your child solves the division problem $20 \div 5 = 4$, then s/he should think whether $4 \times 5 = 20$. If the answer is yes, then the answer to the division problem $7\overline{)70}$ was correct.

Read the problem and choose the best answer. If the answer is not given, choose answer "NH".

Example: $42 \div 6 =$

     a.   36
     b.   7
     c.   8
     d.   NH

The correct answer is "b". $42 \div 6 = 7$.

1. $7 / 1 =$

     a.   6
     b.   8
     c.   7
     d.   NH

2. $9\overline{)36}$

     a.   6
     b.   4
     c.   27
     d.   NH

3. $7\overline{)70}$

     a.   63
     b.   10
     c.   1
     d.   NH

4. $15 \div 3 =$

     a.   12
     b.   5
     c.   3
     d.   NH

5.   Complete the table.

In	Out
8	2
12	3
20	5
16	?

     a.   7
     b.   6
     c.   4
     d.   NH

Content Cluster: COMPUTATION USING SYMBOLIC NOTATION

Subcluster: ADDITION OF WHOLE NUMBERS

Objective: To evaluate knowledge of adding numbers with a place value of 10,000.

Parent Tip: Your third grade child should be able to add or subtract two whole numbers up to 10,000. It is also important to understand that addition and subtraction facts are inversely related. For example, if your child solves the subtraction problem 3,400 - 500 = 2,900, then a simple addition check of 2,900 + 500 = 3,400 will confirm the original answer and help them discover if and where a mistake was made. Remember, it is not just a matter of rewriting the problem backwards, but the inverse problem must be solved as a separate problem to be effective.

Read the problem and choose the best answer. If the answer is not given, choose answer "NH". Don't forget to check your answer.

Example: 7,653 + 7,653 =   <u>Check your work here:</u>

a.	15,306		15,306
b.	14,306		-7,653
c.	15,206		7,653
d.	NH		

The correct answer is "a". 7,653 + 7,653 = 15,306

1.   7,987   <u>Check your work here:</u>
       +2,416

     a.   5,571
     b.   10,403
     c.   10,393
     d.   None of the above

2.   426 + 372 =   <u>Check your work here:</u>

     a.   698
     b.   897
     c.   798
     d.   None of the above

3. $9.06
      + 3.94   Check your work here:

        a. $12.00
        b. $5.12
        c. $13.00
        d.   None of the above

4.   48 + 57 +16 =   Check your work here:

        a.   101
        b.   111
        c.   121
        d.   None of the above

5.   1,382 + 4,916 =   Check your work here:

        a.   5,198
        b.   6,298
        c.   5,298
        d.   None of the above

Content Cluster: COMPUTATION USING SYMBOLIC NOTATION

Subcluster: SUBTRACTION OF WHOLE NUMBERS

Objective: To evaluate knowledge of subtracting numbers with a place value of 10,000.

Parent Tip: For the work in this section, have your child use addition to confirm that the "difference", or answer is correct. If a problem is written horizontally, rewrite the problem vertically and then solve the problem.

Directions: Read the problem and choose the best answer. If the answer is not given, choose answer "NH". Don't forget to check your answer.

Example: $1,272 - 273 =$ Check your work here:

a.	1,545	999
b.	1,000	+ 273
c.	999	1,272
d.	NH	

The correct answer is "c". $1,272 - 273 = 999$ and $999 = 273 = 1,272$

1.   573   Check your work here:
        -264

    a.   209
    b.   309
    c.   837
    d.   NH

2. $0.73 - $0.37 =   Check your work here:

    a. $0.44
    b. $1.10
    c. $0.36
    d.   NH

3.   10,000
        - 4,000   <u>Check your work here:</u>

        a.   6,000
        b.   60,000
        c.   600
        d.   NH

4.   203   <u>Check your work here:</u>
        - 97

        a.   294
        b.   216
        c.   116
        d.   NH

5.   640 – 480 =   <u>Check your work here:</u>

        a.   260
        b.   160
        c.   240
        d.   NH

Content Cluster: COMPUTATION USING SYMBOLIC NOTATION

Subcluster: MULTIPLICATION OF WHOLE NUMBERS

Objective: To evaluate knowledge of multiplying numbers of multiple digits by one digit.

Parent Tip: In this section, your child will use basic multiplication facts to perform larger operations. Before your child can perform these operations, s/he must have mastered the multiplication facts for the numbers between 1 and 10.

Directions: Read the problem and choose the best answer. If the answer is not given, choose answer "NH".

Example: 21 x 6 =

    a.   126
    b.   27
    c.   216
    d.   NH

The correct answer is "a". 21 x 6 = 126

1.   40 x 5 =

    a.   405
    b.   45
    c.   200
    d.   NH

2.   34 x 6 =

    a.   204
    b.   184
    c.   194
    d.   NH

3.   27
        x4

        a.   88
        b.   31
        c.   108
        d.   NH

4.   4,615
        x   2

        a.   8,220
        b.   9,230
        c.   4,617
        d.   NH

5.   314
        x 3

        a.   942
        b.   932
        c.   642
        d.   NH

Content Cluster: COMPUTATION IN CONTEXT

Subcluster: ADDITION AND SUBTRACTION OF WHOLE NUMBERS

Objective: To evaluate knowledge of adding and subtracting whole numbers in word problems.

Parent Tip: Many students are able to perform addition, subtraction, multiplication, and, division problems, but they become confused when the problem is put into context. When your child is doing problems in context, help him/her look for clues that help determine what type of problem s/he is trying to solve. Is it addition, subtraction, division, or multiplication? First decide what to do, then do it, and finally ask if the answer makes sense.

Directions: Read the problem and choose the best answer. If the answer is not given, choose answer "NH".

Example: Mr. Smith's class earned $50 selling candy bars. If they want to buy a new computer game that costs $32, how much money will they have left?

  a. 　$82
  b. 　$18
  c. 　$28
  d. 　NH

The correct answer is "b". $50 - $32 = $18

1. At Monroe Elementary there are 420 students. If 140 of the students are boys, how many are girls?

  a. 　560
  b. 　380
  c. 　280
  d. 　NH

2. How far is it from Mimi's house to her school?

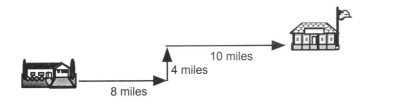

  a. 　22 miles
  b. 　18 miles
  c. 　32 miles
  d. 　NH

Use the following table to answer question 3.

3.   How much farther is it from Los Angeles to New York than from Los Angeles to Denver?

Distance	Miles
Los Angeles to Denver	860
Los Angeles to Atlanta	1,980
Los Angeles to New York	2,670

    a.   1,120 miles
    b.   690 miles
    c.   1,810 miles
    d.   NH

4.   The Jefferson School library had 5,250 books in 1996. In 1997 they bought 1,460 new books, and another 980 new books in 1998. How many books do they have now?

    a.   7,590
    b.   6,690
    c.   7,690
    d.   NH

5.   On a family trip, Miguel counted 17 white cars, 14 red cars, and 11 black cars. How many white and black cars did he count altogether?

    a.   42
    b.   28
    c.   31
    d.   NH

Content Cluster: COMPUTATION IN CONTEXT
Subcluster: ADDITION AND SUBTRACTION OF DECIMALS AND MONEY

Objective: To evaluate knowledge of adding and subtracting decimals in word problems.

Parent Tip: When adding or subtracting decimals or money, always remember to line up the decimals. Also, have your child place the decimal in the answer before solving the problem. That way, the decimal won't be forgotten.

Directions: Read the problem and choose the best answer. If the answer is not given, choose answer "NH".

Example: Felipe has $5.75 that he earned babysitting. He wants to buy two action figures that cost $2.75 each. How much do the action figures cost?

  a. $8.50
  b. $5.50
  c. $3.00
  d. NH

The correct answer is "b". $2.75 + $2.75 = $5.50

1. Josephina needs to buy some supplies for school. If she buys two pencils, two erasers, and one calculator, how much money will she spend?

Josephina's Supplies
Pencil	$0.30
Calculator	$5.00
Eraser	$0.25

  a. $5.55
  b. $6.10
  c. $11.10
  d. NH

2. Billy bought 5.1 gallons of chlorine to put into his parents pool. When he was finished, he had 2.0 gallons left. How much did he use?

  a. 7.1
  b. 3.0
  c. 3.1
  d. NH

3. Omar needed to add 3.2 and .69? What might his answer be?

    a. 389
    b. 10.1
    c. 3.89
    d. NH

4. Sasha earned $20 babysitting. She wanted to buy a video game that costs $21.99. How much more money did she need?

    a. $1.99
    b. $21.99
    c. $20.00
    d. NH

5. A "Walk the Dog" yo-yo costs $3.50, and a "Super Walk the Dog" yo-yo costs $5.10. How much more expensive is the "Super Walk the Dog" yo-yo than the "Walk the Dog" yo-yo?

    a. $2.40
    b. $2.60
    c. $8.60
    d. NH

Content Cluster: COMPUTATION IN CONTEXT
Subcluster: MULTIPLICATION OF WHOLE NUMBERS

Objective: To evaluate knowledge of multiplying whole numbers in word problems.

Parent Tip: Many students are able to perform addition, subtraction, multiplication, and division problems, but they become confused when the problem is put into context. When your child is doing problems in context, help him/her look for clues that help determine what type of problem s/he is trying to solve. Is it addition, subtraction, division, or multiplication? First decide what to do, then do it, and finally ask if the answer makes sense.

Directions: Read the problem and choose the best answer. If the answer is not given, choose answer "NH".

Example: If the flower shop sells a customer ten roses for $3 each, how much money will the order cost?

     a. $7
     b. $13
     c. $30
     d.   NH

The correct answer is "c". 10 x $3 = $30

1.   How much would it cost to buy two hamburgers at Rudy's Grill if each hamburger cost $2?

     a. $4
     b. $6
     c. $5
     d.   NH

2.   The students in Ms. Shelby's class are arranged in five rows. If there are four students per row, how many students are in Ms. Shelby's class?

     a.   20
     b.   9
     c.   25
     d.   NH

3.   The Red Rocket football team scored seven touchdowns in three games. If each touchdown is six points, how many points did they score in all three games?

        a.   21
        b.   18
        c.   20
        d.   NH

4.   Adam practices the piano one hour each day. If he practices for two weeks, how many hours does he practice altogether?

        a.   7
        b.   14
        c.   3
        d.   NH

5.   Kate wants to buy one-half dozen roses. How much money will they cost?

┌─────────────────────────────┐
│   **Flower Sale**   │
│   │
│ $2 each   │
└─────────────────────────────┘

        a. $24
        b. $8
        c. $12
        d.   NH

Content Cluster: ROUNDING

Objective: To evaluate knowledge of number rounding procedures using whole numbers and money.

> **Parent Tip:** Rounding is often confused with estimation. An estimate is more of an approximation, but rounding is a procedure. The rule is that any number is rounded down if it is 0 through 4, and rounded up if it is 5 through 9. Your child is responsible for rounding numbers to the nearest ten, hundred, or dollar. In the following examples, use the underlined digit when rounding to a specific number. To round to the nearest ten, use the ones digit (4_6_). To round to the nearest hundred, use the tens digit (3_8_2). To round to the nearest dollar, use the tenths place ($3._6_1)

Read the problem and choose the best answer. If the answer is not given, choose answer "NH".

Example: Only numbers that are rounded to 200 should be on the inside of the circle, and only numbers that are rounded to 100 should be on the outside of the circle. How many numbers are in the wrong place?

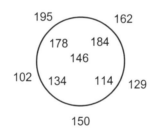

a.	4
b.	5
c.	6
d.	NH

The correct answer is "c". 195, 162, 150, 114, 134, and 146 are in the wrong place.

1. What is $26.50 rounded to the nearest dollar?

    a. $27
    b. $26
    c. $25
    d. NH

2. What is 545 rounded to the nearest ten?

    a. 540
    b. 500
    c. 550
    d. NH

3.   What is 64,716 rounded to the nearest thousand?

        a.   64,000
        b.   64,700
        c.   64,720
        d.   NH

4.   If you round the numbers to the nearest thousand, how many of them would be 7,000?

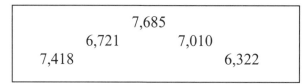

| |
| 7,685 |
| 6,721   7,010 |
| 7,418   6,322 |

        a.   1
        b.   2
        c.   3
        d.   NH

5.   If you round each toy to the nearest dollar, which toys cost $5.00?

Sam's Discount Toys

Item	Price
Doll	$5.95
Stuffed animal	$4.60
Dominos	$5.35

        a.   doll and dominos
        b.   dominos and stuffed animal
        c.   doll and stuffed animal
        d.   NH

ANSWER KEY

Mathematics:
Problem Solving

Concepts of Whole
Numbers
1. b
2. c
3. b
4. a
5. a

Number Sense and
Numeration
1. c
2. c
3. c
4. d
5. b

Geometry and
Spatial Sense
1. c
2. a
3. b
4. b
5. c

Measurement
1. a
2. c
3. d
4. d
5. b

Statistics and
Probability
1. a
2. a

3. c
4. d
5. a

Fraction and
Decimal Concepts
1. a
2. d
3. a
4. d
5. c

Patterns and
Relationships
1. c
2. a
3. a
4. d
5. a

Estimation
1. b
2. b
3. d
4. d
5. b

Mathematics:
Procedures

Multiplication
facts
1. b
2. c
3. c
4. d
5. c

Division Facts
1. c
2. b
3. b
4. b
5. c

Computation
Using Symbolic
Notation

Addition of Whole
Numbers
1. b
2. c
3. c
4. c
5. b

Subtraction of
Whole Numbers
1. b
2. c
3. a
4. d
5. b

Multiplication of
Whole Numbers
1. c
2. a
3. c
4. b
5. a

Computation in
Context

Addition and
Subtraction of
Whole Numbers
1. c
2. a
3. c
4. c
5. b

Addition and
Subtraction of
Decimals and
Money
1. b
2. c
3. c
4. a
5. d

Multiplication of
Whole Numbers
1. a
2. a
3. d
4. b
5. c

Rounding
1. a
2. c
3. d
4. c
5. b

SCIENCE

Content Cluster: EARTH AND SPACE SCIENCE

Objective: To evaluate knowledge of the Earth, it's moon, and how they fit into our solar system.

Parent Tip: Your child should be familiar with the objects in the sky and that they move in predictable patterns. The concept of movement in space and its relation to our earth is a difficult concept for children to understand. Such topics present wonderful opportunities for parents and students to look together in an encyclopedia for information and diagrams clarify these difficult concepts.

Read the problem and choose the best answer

1. Which figure is most probably a moon we would see at night?

 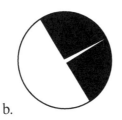 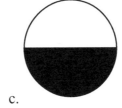 

    a.   b.   c.   d.

    a.   a
    b.   b
    c.   c
    d.   d

2. What instrument would you use to view objects in the sky?

    a.   microscope
    b.   stethoscope
    c.   telescope
    d.   kaleidoscope

3. Which of the following statements is true?

    a.   The earth orbits the moon.
    b.   The moon orbits the earth.
    c.   The sun orbits the earth.
    d.   The sun orbits the moon.

4.   From which direction does the sun rise?
        a.   east
        b.   west
        c.   south
        d.   north

5.   The sun is a large _____
        a.   planet
        b.   asteroid
        c.   moon
        d.   star

6.   Which of the following statements is true?
        a. The Earth is larger than the sun.
        b. The sun is smaller than the moon.
        c. The Earth is larger than the moon.
        d. The moon is larger than the sun.

7.   Which planet is closest to the Earth?
        a. Mercury
        b. Jupiter
        c. Saturn
        d. Mars

8.   Uranus is a unique planet because _____.
        a. it is the largest planet in the solar system
        b. it has "the great red spot"
        c. it is tipped on its side
        d. none of the above

9.   What are comets made of?
        a. gas and fire
        b. dust and ice
        c. gas and dust
        d. dust and fire

10.   Which of the following statements is true?
        a. Mercury is the smallest planet.
        b. The Earth is covered mostly by land.
        c. The sun is not a star.
        d. Some planets are made of gas and some are solid.

Content Cluster: PHYSICAL SCIENCE

Objective: To evaluate knowledge of the forms of matter and their process of change.

Parent Tip: The states of matter – solid, liquid, and gas are important parts of the third grade science standards. You can demonstrate the different states of matter with simple science experiments at home. For example, you can use a glass of water and show how it turns into a solid when it is frozen. This is a great opportunity to introduce your child to the scientific process. You might have your child make a prediction about what s/he thinks will happen, observe what actually happens when the freezing process is finished, and discuss with him/her why the results might have occurred.

Read the problem and choose the best answer.

1.   What process takes place inside the pan as water boils?

    a.   liquid to solid
    b.   solid to gas
    c.   liquid to gas
    d.   gas to solid

2.   Which is not a source of stored energy?

    a.   food
    b.   rock
    c.   fuel
    d.   batteries

3.   All matter is made up of these small particles—

    a.   air
    b.   water
    c.   bones
    d.   atoms

4.   What happens to water when you put it in the freezer?

    a.   it turns into a solid
    b.   it turns into a gas
    c.   it melts
    d.   it evaporates

5.   What happens to the light when it hits the mirror?

        a.   it is refracted
        b.   nothing
        c.   is disappears
        d.   it is reflected

6.   Which of the following items is not a solid?

        a. ice
        b. rock
        c. wood
        d. milk

7. Which of the following is a natural source of light?

        a. lamp
        b. sun
        c. light bulb
        d. flashlight

8. If you put these pictures in order, which picture would be second?

        a. #1
        b. #2
        c. #3
        d. #4

9. Which of the following items is not needed for the plant to grow?

        a. oxygen
        b. sunlight
        c. shade
        d. water

10. Which of the following items would you find on all plants?

        a. roots
        b. leaves
        c. flowers
        d. petals

Content Cluster: LIFE SCIENCE

Objective: To evaluate knowledge of plant life and animal life, and their interactions with the surrounding environment.

Parent Tip: Life science in third grade consists of diverse plant and animal life and the environments where this life might be found. Third graders also learn about the changes that occur when these life forms interact, and what happens to this life when the environment changes. Help your children observe and notice the changes that occur in their daily lives, and continually ask them questions such as why they think this change happened.

Read the problem and choose the best answer.

1.   Which of the following animals is probably a carnivore?

       a.   cow
       b.   sheep
       c.   dog
       d.   horse

2.   Which picture represents an animal that is now extinct?

       a.   b.   c.   d.

       a.   a
       b.   b
       c.   c
       d.   d

3.   A nocturnal animal is one that

       a.   sleeps during the night.
       b.   sleeps during the day.
       c.   eats only plants.
       d.   eats only meat.

4.   Which picture represents plant life that would probably grow where there is little water?

a. 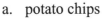   b.   c.   d.

- a.   pine tree
- b.   cactus
- c.   green plant
- d.   rose

5.   How might animal life help plant life grow in the forest?

- a.   the animals don't eat the plants
- b.   the animals die and decay into the soil
- c.   the animals live in the plants
- d.   the animals don't step on the plants

6. Which sense might an eagle rely on to catch its prey?

- a. sight
- b. smell
- c. taste
- d. hearing

7. Noodles are part of which food group?

- a. meats
- b. fruits and vegetables
- c. grains
- d. dairy products

8. Which of the following items might be a healthy snack?

- a. potato chips
- b. apple
- c. fruit punch
- d. soda

9. A balanced meal is made up of foods from all four food groups. Which of the following meals might be a balanced meal?

   a. chicken, rice, salad, and milk
   b. pizza, fruit punch, and carrot sticks
   c. steak, fruit salad, and apple pie
   d. hamburger, fries, and a soda

10. Which of the following animals might be at the top of a food chain?

   a. halibut
   b. seal
   c. shark
   d. lobster

ANSWER KEY

Science

Earth and Space Science
1. a
2. c
3. b
4. a
5. d
6. c
7. d
8. c
9. b
10. d

Physical Science
1. c
2. b
3. d
4. a
5. d
6. d
7. b
8. b
9. c
10. a

Life Science
1. c
2. a
3. b
4. b
5. b
6. a
7. c
8. b
9. a
10. c

SOCIAL SCIENCE

Content Cluster: HISTORY

Objective: To evaluate knowledge of historical events and order.

Parent Tip: Third graders study Native American cultures and settlers who pioneered our country. They also need to have a general idea of the order of our nation's history. One way to learn about history is through reading. A trip to the library can focus on biographies, or even low level history books that might encourage your child's interest in history. These books are often filled with difficult but exciting content and make for a great opportunity for you to read to your child.

Read the problem and choose the best answer. Use the table to answer questions 2 and 3.

1. When the pioneers arrived out west, they staked out land, built their homes, and farmed their land.
2. Life in their new land was not easy for the pioneers. Their days began when the sun came up and ended when the sun went down. Many pioneers went to bed with sore backs from such long days.
3. The pioneers were a brave people. They traveled west in covered wagons. The pioneers faced danger, uncertainty, severe weather conditions, and even illness and death.

1.   To write a story from the above chart, what would be the best order for these sentences?

    a.   1, 2, 3
    b.   2, 3, 1
    c.   3, 2, 1
    d.   3, 1, 2

2.   Judging from the chart, what kind of person would not make a good pioneer?

    a.   frail
    b.   adventurous
    c.   strong
    d.   hearty

3.   Native Americans lived in which part of the United States?

    a.   Northwest
    b.   Southwest
    c.   Central Plains
    d.   All of the above

4.   Which was probably not a source of food for the Native Americans?

    a.   water
    b.   buffalo
    c.   salmon
    d.   electricity

5.   Which of these people was probably born second?

    a.   George Washington
    b.   Abe Lincoln
    c.   Bill Clinton
    d.   George Bush

6.   Which of the following items is not a natural resource for the Native Americans?

    a. leather
    b. wood
    c. fish
    d. glass

7.   The early settlers moved out west by _____?

    a. train
    b. horse
    c. covered wagon
    d. automobile

8.   George Washington is famous because _____.

    a. he wrote the Declaration of Independence
    b. he freed the slaves
    c. he was the first President of the United States
    d. he shouted "The British are Coming!"

9.   Prior to the American Revolution, who ruled the American colonies?

    a. Canada
    b. England
    c. Fance
    d. Mexico

10.   In what famous city did the colonists throw tea into the ocean?

    a. Plymouth
    b. New York
    c. Philadelphia
    d. Boston

Content Cluster: GEOGRAPHY

Objective: To evaluate knowledge of map reading and the Earth's geography

Parent Tip: In previous grades, your child became familiar with the local geography. Your child should now be familiar with the geography of the United States, as well as the concept of the earth as seen on a globe. Such spatial concepts are difficult for your child to understand, and the use of manipulatives would be a great help. For example, build a puzzle of the United States with your child to familiarize him/her with the geography of the states.

Read the problem and choose the best answer. Use the United States map to answer questions 1 and 2, and use the globe to answer questions 4 and 5.

1.   Which two states would be the farthest south in the continental United States?

    a.   Alaska and Hawaii
    b.   California and Florida
    c.   Florida and Texas
    d.   California and Texas

2.   Which state is east of the shaded state?

    a.   Oregon
    b.   Idaho
    c.   Washington
    d.   California

3.   Which of these statements is true?

    a. Los Angeles is north of San Francisco
    b. San Francisco is south of San Diego
    c. San Diego is north of Los Angeles
    d. Los Angeles is north of San Diego

4.   Is the equator a line of longitude or latitude?

    a. longitude
    b. latitude
    c. both
    d. neither

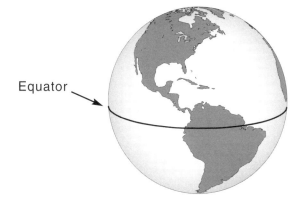

Equator

5.   According to the globe, where would you find the United States?

    a. the South Pole
    b. the North Pole
    c. the Northern Hemisphere
    d. the Southern Hemisphere

6.   According to the globe, which continent is entirely south of the equator?

    a. Africa
    b. North America
    c. South America
    d. Australia

7.   If you were standing in the middle of the United States and traveled west, which state might you run into?

    a. Louisiana
    b. Nevada
    c. Tennessee
    d. Michigan

8. Which state is the largest state in the continental United States?

    a. Alaska
    b. California
    c. New York
    d. Texas

9. What country borders the United States to the north?

    a. Mexico
    b. Alaska
    c. Canada
    d. Antarctica

10. Which two cities listed below are state capitals?

    a. New York City and Austin
    b. Los Angeles and Albany
    c. Sacramento and Seattle
    d. Albany and Sacramento

Content Cluster: CIVICS AND GOVERNMENT

Objective: To evaluate knowledge of citizens and government interaction.

> **Parent Tip:** Our government has rules and consequences, and so does a family. Use the newspaper or television news to help your child understand the importance of rules and consequences, and show how the government and the family are alike in many ways. Each member of a family has a specific job, responsibilities, and specific rules to follow.

Directions: Read the problem and choose the best answer.

1.   Classrooms in schools have rules, and so does our government. Which of the ideas might not be a reason why there are rules?

    a.   to protect peoples' rights
    b.   to provide order
    c.   to have consequences
    d.   to make sure responsibilities are carried out

2.   In most cases, if a person wants to hold a government office, s/he <u>must</u> _____.

    a.   be old
    b.   be elected
    c.   have lots of money
    d.   be honest

3.   Which of these people might be citizens of the United States?

    a.   a senator
    b.   a teacher
    c.   a student
    d.   all of the above

4.   Which person is elected to run a state?

    a.   Councilperson
    b.   Mayor
    c.   Governor
    d.   Senator

5.   Which person is elected to run the United States?

     a.   Mayor
     b.   Governor
     c.   President
     d.   Chief of Police

6.   Which of the following items is not a political party of the United States?

     a. Republican
     b. Conservative
     c. Independent
     d. Democrat

7. The President of the United States lives in the _____.

     a. Pentagon
     b. Smithsonian
     c. Washington Monument
     d. White House

8. In the United States the people vote for a new president every _____ years.

     a. two
     b. four
     c. three
     d. five

9. To become President of the United States, you must _____.

     a. be a man
     b. be a citizen
     c. be wealthy
     d. be married

10. Where is the capitol of the United States located?

     a. Washington
     b. Sacramento
     c. Washington D.C.
     d. Tacoma

Content Cluster: ECONOMICS

Objective: To evaluate knowledge of consumer goods and their relative values.

Parent Tip: Every time you go to the supermarket or a specialty store, make it an educational trip. Point out that each item has a value, and find out where that item was made. Was it made locally, somewhere else in the United States, or out of the country? What is the price of the item? Is it the cheapest option, or might there be a cheaper or better alternative? As you begin this process, the best way to do this is to communicate with your child throughout the shopping trip. Explain to him/her why you choose certain brands over others.

Directions: Read the problem and choose the best answer.

1.   When a person wants to make a profit, they should do which of the following?

        a.   Sell the item for less than it cost.
        b.   Buy the item and give it away for free.
        c.   Sell the item for more than it cost.
        d.   Sell the item for the same price it cost.

Use the following chart to answer questions 2 through 5.

Item	Friday's Regular Price	Saturday's Sale Price
Baseball cards	$1.50	$0.99
Model airplane	$5.00	$3.49
Race car	$7.00	$5.49

2.   Mike earned $10 and wants to spend it at the toy store. How could Mike get the most for his money?

        a.   Mike should buy the race car and the baseball cards on Friday.
        b.   Mike should buy the model airplane and baseball cards on Friday.
        c.   Mike should buy the race car and model airplane on Friday.
        d.   Mike should wait for the sale on Saturday.

3.   Jonah is on a tight budget this month and doesn't have much money to spend. Which item would be the most important for Jonah to buy?

        a.   a computer
        b.   a car
        c.   food
        d.   a pet

4.   If Mike has $13.50 to spend at the toy store, how should he spend his money?

    a. Buy one of each toy on Friday.
    b. Buy two baseball cards and two model airplanes on Friday.
    c. Buy two of each toy on Saturday.
    d. Spend all $13.50 on Saturday.

5.   What might be a reason why Mike could not buy all three toys on Friday?

    a. The toys were too expensive
    b. He has to pay sales tax on the toys
    c. The toys are not on sale on Friday
    d. He must wait for Saturday's sale

Use the following graph to answer questions 6 through 8.

6.   Larry sells watermelon in California. He can order the watermelon from each of the countries on the graph. Where should Larry buy his watermelon if he wants to buy it and then sell it for less than $2 per pound?

    a.   U.S.A.
    b.   Mexico
    c.   Brazil
    d.   Canada

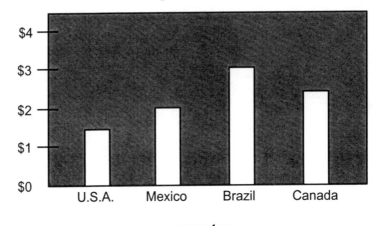

Watermelon Producing Countries Price Graph

country

7.   Which country would be the last place where Larry would choose to buy his watermelon?

    a.   U.S.A.
    b.   Mexico
    c.   Brazil
    d.   Canada

8. What would happen to the price of watermelon in the U.S.A. if this year's crop is much lower than expected?

    a. The price of watermelon in the U.S.A. would probably increase.
    b. The price of watermelon in the U.S.A. would probably decrease.
    c. The price of watermelon in the U.S.A. would stay the same.
    d. It is impossible to tell without more information.

9. What could the owner of a hot dog stand do if he wants to increase the number of people who buy from his stand?

    a. Sell smaller hot dogs.
    b. Raise the price of hot dogs.
    c. Lower the price of hot dogs.
    d. Charge extra money for catsup and mustard.

10. Mina wants to paint her friends' nails to make money. A simple manicure takes her 20 minutes and a fancy manicure takes her 30 minutes. If she charges three dollars for a simple manicure and five dollars for a fancy manicure, how would she make the most money in one hour?

    a. Two simple manicures
    b. Two fancy manicures
    c. Three simple manicures
    d. Three fancy manicures

Content Cluster: CULTURE

Objective: To evaluate knowledge of the concepts of family and community, and how they affect each other.

> **Parent Tip:** Help your children understand that the basic concept of culture for third graders is their community. Help point out that everything from their sports team, their class at school, their family, their church, and their neighborhood are all part of their community. Most importantly, point out that they can belong to several groups at once within their community.

Read the problem and choose the best answer.

1. The Cheyenne people had to follow the buffalo for food. What type of house would this Native American tribe most likely use?

    a. long house
    b. pueblo
    c. tepee
    d. hogan

2. This Native American pottery is made of red clay. Where might this Native American tribe have lived?

    a. the plains
    b. the desert
    c. the pacific coast
    d. the northeastern woodlands

3. In the United States many people celebrate Martin Luther King Jr. Day. What do you think is the best reason this day became an official holiday?

    a. to get an extra day off school
    b. to honor a man who died
    c. to help remember a hard working man
    d. to honor a man who sought equality for all people

4.   Family was a large part of the Native American community. Which of the following might not be considered part of your community?

    a.   your church
    b.   your state
    c.   your family
    d.   your school

5.   From which of the following regions did Native American people build totem poles as part of their culture?

    a.   the plains
    b.   the desert
    c.   the Pacific coast
    d   the Northeastern woodlands

6. Which Native American group were excellent fishermen?

    a. the plains
    b. the desert
    c. the Pacific coast
    d. the Northeastern woodlands

7. How were Native American men and women different?

    a. Men did the cooking, and women did the fishing.
    b. Women did the hunting, and men did the fishing.
    c. Women did the fishing, and men did the weaving.
    d. Women did the weaving, and men did the hunting.

8. Native Americans often told stories to honor an important person. Which of the following items is a tribute to an important person today?

    a. The White House
    b. The Lincoln Memorial
    c. The Pentagon
    d. Capital Hill

9. Which of the following is not a way we honor important people in our society today?

    a. name a street after the person
    b. make a person pay a fine
    c. erect a statue of the person
    d. tell stories about the person

10. If a person in a community needs help, who would be able to help him?

    a. the police
    b. a friend
    c. a doctor
    d. all of the above

ANSWER KEY

Social Science

History
1. d
2. a
3. d
4. d
5. b
6. d
7. c
8. c
9. b
10. d

Geography
1. c
2. b
3. d
4. b
5. c
6. c
7. b
8. d
9. c
10. d

Civics and Government
1. c
2. b
3. d
4. c

5. c
6. b
7. d
8. b
9. b
10. c

Economics
1. c
2. d
3. c
4. d
5. b
6. a
7. c
8. a
9. c
10. b

Culture
1. c
2. b
3. d
4. b
5. c
6. c
7. d
8. b
9. b
10. d